My First Poem

Eastern Scotland

Edited By Jenni Harrison

First published in Great Britain in 2017 by:

Young Writers
Coltsfoot Drive
Peterborough
PE2 9BF
Telephone: 01733 890066
Website: www.youngwriters.co.uk

Foreword

Young Writers was established in 1991 with the aim of
encouraging writing skills in young people and giving
them the opportunity to see their work in print. Poetry is a
wonderful way to introduce young children to the idea of
rhyme and rhythm and helps learning and development
of communication, language and literacy skills.
'My First Poem' was created to introduce nursery and
preschool children to this wonderful world of poetry.
They were given a template to fill in with their own words,
creating a poem that was all about them.
We are proud to present the resulting collection
of personal and touching poems in this anthology,
which can be treasured for years to come.

Jenni Bannister

Editorial Manager

Contents

Lossiemouth Childcare Centre, Lossiemouth

Samuel Edwards (4)	52
Henry Duncan Lambert (3)	53
Angus Michael Elliott (4)	54
Finlay Dodds (4)	55
Maya Natasha Herrity (4)	56
Harley James (3)	57
Jack Moore (4)	58
Lucy Connie Jackson (3)	59
Koa Fenwick (3)	60
Harrison Jack May (4)	61
Katie Louise Bell (4)	62
Ellie Iris Ralston (4)	63
Freya Rose Gresswell Grant (4)	64
Arran Ritchie (3)	65
Blake Philip (4)	66
Joseph McIntosh (4)	67
Lily Robinson (3)	68
Nieve Elizabeth Smith (4)	69
Harry Williams (4)	70
Ava Lynne Midgley (4)	71
Isla Jayne Simpson (4)	72
Jack Dobson (3)	73
Lilja Gowanlock (4)	74
Ellie Handford (4)	75
Leo Morton (3)	76
Isabella Gandy (4)	77
Jessica Murray (3)	78
Oscar Renison (4)	79
Max Wainwright (3)	80
Ryan Denoon (3)	81
Archie Dempsey (3)	82
Lacey Jane Goodwin (4)	83
Logan Cooper (3)	84
Joshua Joyce (3)	85
Archie Griffiths (4)	86
Aiden Johnstone (4)	87

Pitreavie Playgroup, Dunfermline

Amber Swanson (3)	88
Matthew Douglas Codona (4)	89
Charlotte Harker (2)	90
Amelia Sallnow (3)	91
Euan Love (3)	92

Torphins Playgroup, Banchory

Arran Stewart McGeachie (2)	93
Brodie Davidson (2)	94
Charlotte Lockwood (3)	95
Findlay Boyd (2)	96
Imogen Robertson (2)	97
Zara Shepherd (3)	98
Daisy Eleanor Newman (3)	99
Kian Allan (3)	100
Fergus McCallum (2)	101
Eloise Fulton (2)	102
Jessica Gray (2)	103
Callum Jamie Yule (3)	104

The Poems

Lacie's First Poem

My name is Lacie and I go to preschool,

My best friends are Liam and Granny, who are

really cool.

I watch Peppa Pig on TV,

Playing and drawing pictures is lots of fun for me.

I just love pasta to eat,

And sometimes cake for a treat.

Pink is a colour I like a lot,

My pig is the best present I ever got.

My favourite person is Mummy, who is a gem,

So this, my first poem, is just for them!

Lacie Julie Messenger (2)

Acorn Day Nursery, St Andrews

Connaire's First Poem

My name is Connaire and I go to preschool,

My best friend is Callan, who is really cool.

I watch PAW Patrol on TV,

Playing and drawing pictures is lots of fun for me.

I just love pasta to eat,

And sometimes cake for a treat.

Black is a colour I like a lot,

My pencils are the best present I ever got.

My favourite person is Mummy, who is a gem,

So this, my first poem, is just for them!

Connaire Rouget (3)

Acorn Day Nursery, St Andrews

Holly's First Poem

My name is Holly and I go to preschool,

My best friend is Jamie, who is really cool.

I watch PJ Masks on TV,

Playing and making at the art table is lots of fun

for me.

I just love pizza to eat,

And sometimes chocolate for a treat.

Blue is a colour I like a lot,

My wolf is the best present I ever got.

My favourite person is my sister, who is a gem,

So this, my first poem, is just for them!

Holly Anderson (4)

Acorn Day Nursery, St Andrews

Ben's First Poem

My name is **Ben** and I go to preschool,

My best friend is **Orlaith**, who is really cool.

I watch **Ice Age** on TV,

Playing **Woody** is lots of fun for me.

I just love **pasta** to eat,

And sometimes **I eat biscuits** for a treat.

Red is a colour I like a lot,

My **PAW Patrol pups** are the best present I ever got.

My favourite person is **Charlie**, who is a gem,

So this, my first poem, is just for them!

Ben Lothian (3)

Acorn Day Nursery, St Andrews

Jenny's First Poem

My name is Jenny and I go to preschool,
My best friend is Ruby, who is really cool.
I watch Peppa Pig on TV,
Playing in the home corner is lots of fun for me.
I just love macaroni to eat,
And sometimes a biscuit for a treat.
Pink is a colour I like a lot,
My Busy Bee is the best present I ever got.
My favourite person is George, who is a gem,
So this, my first poem, is just for them!

Jenny Agnes Wilson (4)
Acorn Day Nursery, St Andrews

Orlaith's First Poem

My name is Orlaith Lawson and I go to preschool,
My best friend is Eleanor, who is really cool.
I watch PAW Patrol on TV,
Playing with George is lots of fun for me.
I just love pasta to eat,
And sometimes sweeties for a treat.
Pink is a colour I like a lot,
My George is the best present I ever got.
My favourite person is Sally, who is a gem,
So this, my first poem, is just for them!

Orlaith Lawson (3)

Acorn Day Nursery, St Andrews

Faizaan's First Poem

My name is Faizaan and I go to preschool,

My best friend is Lewis, who is really cool.

I watch everything on TV,

Playing on my scooter is lots of fun for me.

I just love blueberries and lollipops to eat,

And sometimes ice cream with Smarties for

a treat.

Rainbow is a colour I like a lot,

My remote-controlled car is the best present I

ever got.

My favourite person is Mummy, who is a gem,

So this, my first poem, is just for them!

Faizaan Zohaib Ullah (4)

Clever Clogs Childcare Centre, Kelty

Kadyn's First Poem

My name is **Kadyn** and I go to preschool,

My best friends are **Mummy and Daddy**, who are
really cool.

I watch **PAW Patrol** on TV,

Playing **with my doggy** is lots of fun for me.

I just love **apples** to eat,

And sometimes **sweeties** for a treat.

Black and blue are colours I like a lot,

My **jigsaw puzzle** is the best present I ever got.

My favourite person is **Stuart**, who is a gem,

So this, my first poem, is just for them!

Kadyn Calder (3)

Clever Clogs Childcare Centre, Kelty

Betsie's First Poem

My name is **Betsie** and I go to preschool,
My best friend is **Millie**, who is really cool.
I watch **Peter Rabbit** on TV,
Playing **with my bunny** is lots of fun for me.
I just love **sausages** to eat,
And sometimes **sweeties** for a treat.
Pink is a colour I like a lot,
My **look-out and air patroller** are the best
presents I ever got.
My favourite person is **Mummy**, who is a gem,
So this, my first poem, is just for them!

Betsie Boo Burns (3)

Clever Clogs Childcare Centre, Kelty

Emma's First Poem

My name is **Emma** and I go to preschool,
My best friend is **Julia**, who is really cool.
I watch **My Little Pony** on TV,
Playing **on my princess tablet** is lots of fun for me.
I just love **sausages** to eat,
And sometimes **popcorn** for a treat.
Silver and gold are colours I like a lot,
My **tablet** is the best present I ever got.
My favourite person is **Katie**, who is a gem,
So this, my first poem, is just for them!

Emma Duncan (4)
Clever Clogs Childcare Centre, Kelty

Cameron's First Poem

My name is Cameron and I go to preschool,

My best friends are everybody, who are really cool.

I watch Tom and Jerry on TV,

Playing with my dinosaurs is lots of fun for me.

I just love apples to eat,

And sometimes chocolate for a treat.

Blue is a colour I like a lot,

My cars are the best present I ever got.

My favourite person is Mummy, who is a gem,

So this, my first poem, is just for them!

Cameron Baillie (4)

Clever Clogs Childcare Centre, Kelty

Jack's First Poem

My name is Jack and I go to preschool,

My best friend is Matthew, who is really cool.

I watch Star Wars on TV,

Playing with my teddy is lots of fun for me.

I just love meatballs to eat,

And sometimes sweets for a treat.

Green is a colour I like a lot,

My remote-controlled helicopter is the best

present I ever got.

My favourite person is Cameron, who is a gem,

So this, my first poem, is just for them!

Jack Bell

Clever Clogs Childcare Centre, Kelty

Harrison's First Poem

My name is Harrison and I go to preschool,
My best friend is Mummy, who is really cool.
I watch racing cars on TV,
Playing outside is lots of fun for me.
I just love doughnuts to eat,
And sometimes sweets for a treat.
Blue and green are colours I like a lot,
My Hot Wheels garage is the best present I ever got.
My favourite person is Daddy, who is a gem,
So this, my first poem, is just for them!

Harrison Mason
Clever Clogs Childcare Centre, Kelty

Faith's First Poem

My name is **Faith** and I go to preschool,

My best friends are **Heidi and Summer**, who are

really cool.

I watch **racing cars** on TV,

Playing **with my toys** is lots of fun for me.

I just love **sausages** to eat,

And sometimes **sweeties** for a treat.

Pink is a colour I like a lot,

My **bike** is the best present I ever got.

My favourite person is **Mummy**, who is a gem,

So this, my first poem, is just for them!

Faith Mitchell (3)

Clever Clogs Childcare Centre, Kelty

Caolila-Alba's First Poem

My name is Caolila-Alba Thomson and I go to preschool,

My best friend is Ava, who is really cool.

I watch Go Jetters on TV,

Playing with my cat is lots of fun for me.

I just love carrots to eat,

And sometimes sweeties for a treat.

Orange is a colour I like a lot,

My bicycle is the best present I ever got.

My favourite person is Granny, who is a gem,

So this, my first poem, is just for them!

Caolila-Alba Thomson (3)

Clever Clogs Childcare Centre, Kelty

Rudi's First Poem

My name is **Rudi** and I go to preschool,

My best friend is **Jamie**, who is really cool.

I watch **PAW Patrol** on TV,

Playing **with my cars** is lots of fun for me.

I just love **sausages** to eat,

And sometimes **chocolate** for a treat.

Blue is a colour I like a lot,

My **Ninja Turtles** are the best present I ever got.

My favourite person is **Mummy**, who is a gem,

So this, my first poem, is just for them!

Rudi MacDonald (3)

Clever Clogs Childcare Centre, Kelty

Kyle's First Poem

My name is **Kyle** and I go to preschool,

My best friend is **Alex**, who is really cool.

I watch **Tom and Jerry** on TV,

Playing **with Thomas trains** is lots of fun for me.

I just love **toast** to eat,

And sometimes **sweeties** for a treat.

Blue is a colour I like a lot,

My **Thomas train** is the best present I ever got.

My favourite person is **Mummy**, who is a gem,

So this, my first poem, is just for them!

Kyle Sutherland (4)

Clever Clogs Childcare Centre, Kelty

Lexi's First Poem

My name is Lexi and I go to preschool,
My best friend is Amelia, who is really cool.
I watch Shimmer and Shine on TV,
Playing doggy is lots of fun for me.
I just love cheeseburgers to eat,
And sometimes lollipops for a treat.
Pink is a colour I like a lot,
My scooter is the best present I ever got.
My favourite person is Charlie, who is a gem,
So this, my first poem, is just for them!

Lexi Strachan (4)
Clever Clogs Childcare Centre, Kelty

Darci's First Poem

My name is Darci and I go to preschool,
My best friend is Ruby, who is really cool.
I watch Peppa Pig on TV,
Playing Doc McStuffins is lots of fun for me.
I just love spaghetti to eat,
And sometimes a biscuit for a treat.
Brown is a colour I like a lot,
My black tablet is the best present I ever got.
My favourite person is Ruby, who is a gem,
So this, my first poem, is just for them!

Darci Davies (3)
Clever Clogs Childcare Centre, Kelty

Sol's First Poem

My name is Sol and I go to preschool,

My best friend is Markus, who is really cool.

I watch Peppa Pig on TV,

Playing with my dinosaurs is lots of fun for me.

I just love pasta to eat,

And sometimes sweeties for a treat.

Orange is a colour I like a lot,

My big dinosaur is the best present I ever got.

My favourite person is Mummy, who is a gem,

So this, my first poem, is just for them!

Sol Mair (3)

Clever Clogs Childcare Centre, Kelty

Ruby's First Poem

My name is Ruby and I go to preschool,
My best friend is Daddy, who is really cool.
I watch Peppa Pig on TV,
Playing with my baby is lots of fun for me.
I just love soup to eat,
And sometimes biscuits for a treat.
Pink is a colour I like a lot,
My princess toys are the best present I ever got.
My favourite person is Mummy, who is a gem,
So this, my first poem, is just for them!

Ruby Easton (3)
Clever Clogs Childcare Centre, Kelty

Adam's First Poem

My name is Adam and I go to preschool,

My best friend is Sophie, who is really cool.

I watch PAW Patrol on TV,

Playing with my trains is lots of fun for me.

I just love pasta to eat,

And sometimes biscuits for a treat.

White is a colour I like a lot,

My motorbike is the best present I ever got.

My favourite person is Mummy, who is a gem,

So this, my first poem, is just for them!

Adam Kinnersley (3)

Clever Clogs Childcare Centre, Kelty

Jayden's First Poem

My name is Jayden and I go to preschool,
My best friend is Daddy, who is really cool.
I watch Go Jetters on TV,
Playing outside is lots of fun for me.
I just love bananas to eat,
And sometimes a biscuit for a treat.
Blue is a colour I like a lot,
My cars are the best present I ever got.
My favourite person is Mummy, who is a gem,
So this, my first poem, is just for them!

Jayden Bennie (4)
Clever Clogs Childcare Centre, Kelty

Daniel's First Poem

My name is **Daniel** and I go to preschool,
My best friend is **Adam**, who is really cool.
I watch **PAW Patrol** on TV,
Playing **football** is lots of fun for me.
I just love **sausages** to eat,
And sometimes **biscuits** for a treat.
Blue is a colour I like a lot,
My **cars** are the best present I ever got.
My favourite person is **Mummy**, who is a gem,
So this, my first poem, is just for them!

Daniel Stuart King (3)

Clever Clogs Childcare Centre, Kelty

Brandon's First Poem

My name is Brandon and I go to preschool,
My best friend is Daddy, who is really cool.
I watch PAW Patrol on TV,
Playing with my cars is lots of fun for me.
I just love sausages to eat,
And sometimes sweeties for a treat.
Blue is a colour I like a lot,
My bike is the best present I ever got.
My favourite person is Mummy, who is a gem,
So this, my first poem, is just for them!

Brandon Millar (4)
Clever Clogs Childcare Centre, Kelty

Airlie's First Poem

My name is **Airlie** and I go to preschool,
My best friend is **Sol**, who is really cool.
I watch **Peppa** on TV,
Playing **with my toy car** is lots of fun for me.
I just love **peas** to eat,
And sometimes **sweeties** for a treat.
Pink is a colour I like a lot,
My **toy kitchen** is the best present I ever got.
My favourite person is **Aspen**, who is a gem,
So this, my first poem, is just for them!

Airlie Green (3)
Clever Clogs Childcare Centre, Kelty

Markus' First Poem

My name is **Markus** and I go to preschool,
My best friend is **Sol**, who is really cool.
I watch **Cars** on TV,
Playing **with my cars** is lots of fun for me.
I just love **potatoes** to eat,
And sometimes **sweeties** for a treat.
Blue is a colour I like a lot,
My **cars** are the best present I ever got.
My favourite person is **Mummy**, who is a gem,
So this, my first poem, is just for them!

Markus Wiczynski (3)

Clever Clogs Childcare Centre, Kelty

Sophie's First Poem

My name is Sophie and I go to preschool,
My best friend is Tilly, who is really cool.
I watch Peppa Pig on TV,
Playing on my bed is lots of fun for me.
I just love potatoes to eat,
And sometimes sweeties for a treat.
Pink is a colour I like a lot,
My dolly is the best present I ever got.
My favourite person is Mummy, who is a gem,
So this, my first poem, is just for them!

Sophie Fraser (3)
Clever Clogs Childcare Centre, Kelty

Bryanna's First Poem

My name is **Bryanna** and I go to preschool,
My best friend is **Ruby**, who is really cool.
I watch **Peppa Pig** on TV,
Playing **with my babies** is lots of fun for me.
I just love **pasta** to eat,
And sometimes **pizza** for a treat.
Red is a colour I like a lot,
My **scooter** is the best present I ever got.
My favourite person is **Mummy**, who is a gem,
So this, my first poem, is just for them!

Bryanna Joy Davina Hunter (3)
Clever Clogs Childcare Centre, Kelty

Max's First Poem

My name is Max and I go to preschool,
My best friend is Muir, who is really cool.
I watch PAW Patrol on TV,
Playing choo-choo games is lots of fun for me.
I just love pizza to eat,
And sometimes chocolate for a treat.
Green is a colour I like a lot,
My car is the best present I ever got.
My favourite person is Muir, who is a gem,
So this, my first poem, is just for them!

Max Innes (3)
Clever Clogs Childcare Centre, Kelty

Seb's First Poem

My name is **Seb** and I go to preschool,

My best friend is **Callum**, who is really cool.

I watch **Go Jetters** on TV,

Playing **outside** is lots of fun for me.

I just love **toast** to eat,

And sometimes **sweeties** for a treat.

Blue is a colour I like a lot,

My **scooter** is the best present I ever got.

My favourite person is **Daddy**, who is a gem,

So this, my first poem, is just for them!

Seb Fleming (4)

Clever Clogs Childcare Centre, Kelty

Logan's First Poem

My name is Logan and I go to preschool,

My best friend is Jayden, who is really cool.

I watch PAW Patrol on TV,

Playing chase is lots of fun for me.

I just love pizza to eat,

And sometimes biscuits for a treat.

Blue is a colour I like a lot,

My scooter is the best present I ever got.

My favourite person is Daddy, who is a gem,

So this, my first poem, is just for them!

Logan Jack Hutton (3)
Clever Clogs Childcare Centre, Kelty

Mason's First Poem

My name is Mason and I go to preschool,
My best friend is Myles, who is really cool.
I watch Toy Story on TV,
Playing Minions is lots of fun for me.
I just love cereal to eat,
And sometimes biscuits for a treat.
Blue is a colour I like a lot,
My Batman is the best present I ever got.
My favourite person is Daddy, who is a gem,
So this, my first poem, is just for them!

Mason Linton (3)
Clever Clogs Childcare Centre, Kelty

Sophie's First Poem

My name is Sophie Reid and I go to preschool,

My best friend is Clara, who is really cool.

I watch PAW Patrol on TV,

Playing with my pet guinea pigs is lots of fun

for me.

I just love sausages to eat,

And sometimes pancakes for a treat.

Pink is a colour I like a lot,

My Baby Annabell and pram are the best presents

I ever got.

My favourite person is Adriana (my cousin), who is

a gem,

So this, my first poem, is just for them!

Sophie Reid (3)

Ferryfield Playgroup, Cupar

Riley's First Poem

My name is Riley and I go to preschool,
My best friend is Connor, who is really cool.
I watch Transformers Rescue Bots on TV,
Playing with Sion and Isla is lots of fun for me.
I just love raspberries and blueberries to eat,
And sometimes jelly beans for a treat.
Blue is a colour I like a lot,
My easel is the best present I ever got.
My favourite person is my daddy, who is a gem,
So this, my first poem, is just for them!

Riley Benjamin Pepper (2)

Ferryfield Playgroup, Cupar

Millie's First Poem

My name is **Millie Harris** and I go to preschool,
My best friend is **Bella**, who is really cool.
I watch **Peppa Pig and Ben and Holly** on TV,
Playing **with my doll's house** is lots of fun for me.
I just love **pizza** to eat,
And sometimes **cookies** for a treat.
Orange is a colour I like a lot,
My **Peppa kitchen** is the best present I ever got.
My favourite person is **Grandad**, who is a gem,
So this, my first poem, is just for them!

Millie Niamh Harris (2)

Ferryfield Playgroup, Cupar

Mya-Louise's First Poem

My name is Mya-Louise Fearson and I go
to preschool,
My best friends are Grace and Archie, who are
really cool.
I watch Trolls on TV.
Playing with my toys is lots of fun for me.
I just love carrots to eat,
And sometimes popcorn for a treat.
Pink is a colour I like a lot,
My Marshall is the best present I ever got.
My favourite person is Grace, who is a gem,
So this, my first poem, is just for them!

Mya-Louise Frearson (3)

Ferryfield Playgroup, Cupar

Ruva's First Poem

My name is **Ruva** and I go to preschool,

My best friend is **Grace**, who is really cool.

I watch **The Winx** on TV,

Playing **houses** is lots of fun for me.

I just love **fish and chips with ketchup** to eat,

And sometimes **special chocolate** for a treat.

Red is a colour I like a lot,

My **tea trolley** is the best present I ever got.

My favourite person is **Daddy**, who is a gem,

So this, my first poem, is just for them!

Ruva Magumise (4)

Ferryfield Playgroup, Cupar

Cora's First Poem

My name is Cora and I go to preschool,

My best friend is Eliana, who is really cool.

I watch My Little Pony on TV,

Playing dressing up is lots of fun for me.

I just love chocolate cake to eat,

And sometimes ice cream for a treat.

Pink is a colour I like a lot,

My Archie puppet dog is the best present I ever got.

My favourite person is Erin, who is a gem,

So this, my first poem, is just for them!

Cora Rose Mccann (3)

Ferryfield Playgroup, Cupar

Clara's First Poem

My name is Clara and I go to preschool,

My best friend is Sophie, who is really cool.

I watch PAW Patrol on TV,

Playing with Sophie is lots of fun for me.

I just love macaroni to eat,

And sometimes ice cream for a treat.

Pink is a colour I like a lot,

My doll's house is the best present I ever got.

My favourite person is Mummy, who is a gem,

So this, my first poem, is just for them!

Clara Daisy Ho-A-Yun (3)

Ferryfield Playgroup, Cupar

Talia's First Poem

My name is **Talia** and I go to preschool,
My best friend is **Jake**, who is really cool.
I watch **Peppa Pig** on TV,
Playing **outside** is lots of fun for me.
I just love **strawberries** to eat,
And sometimes **ice lollies** for a treat.
Blue is a colour I like a lot,
My **unicorn** is the best present I ever got.
My favourite person is **Mummy**, who is a gem,
So this, my first poem, is just for them!

Talia Smart (4)
Ferryfield Playgroup, Cupar

Zak's First Poem

My name is **Zak** and I go to preschool,
My best friend is **Kyle**, who is really cool.
I watch **Postman Pat** on TV,
Playing **shops** is lots of fun for me.
I just love **crackers and cheese** to eat,
And sometimes **cake** for a treat.
Green is a colour I like a lot,
My **Buzz Lightyear** is the best present I ever got.
My favourite person is **Granny**, who is a gem,
So this, my first poem, is just for them!

Zak Tait (2)

Ferryfield Playgroup, Cupar

Sophie's First Poem

My name is Sophie and I go to preschool,
My best friend is Clara, who is really cool.
I watch Peppa Pig on TV,
Playing with my dolly is lots of fun for me.
I just love fish to eat,
And sometimes sweeties for a treat.
Green as grass is a colour I like a lot,
My LeapPad is the best present I ever got.
My favourite person is Granny, who is a gem,
So this, my first poem, is just for them!

Sophie Gourley (2)
Ferryfield Playgroup, Cupar

Taylor's First Poem

My name is **Taylor** and I go to preschool,

My best friend is **Daniel**, who is really cool.

I watch **programmes** on TV,

Playing **PAW Patrol and princesses** is lots of fun
for me.

I just love **raisins, grapes and strawberries**
to eat,

And sometimes **ice cream** for a treat.

Pink is a colour I like a lot,

My **Boo (little soft toy dog)** is the best present I
ever got.

My favourite person is **Mummy**, who is a gem,

So this, my first poem, is just for them!

Taylor Sienna Moore (3)

Knockando Playgroup, Aberlour

Daniel's First Poem

My name is Daniel Richard and I go to preschool,

My best friends are Christopher, Jack and Sam,

who are really cool.

I watch PAW Patrol on TV,

Playing Pig Goes Pop is lots of fun for me.

I just love a Hawaiian pizza to eat,

And sometimes sweeties for a treat.

Blue is a colour I like a lot,

My PAW Patrol playset is the best present I

ever got.

My favourite person is Dad, who is a gem,

So this, my first poem, is just for them!

Daniel Richard (4)

Knockando Playgroup, Aberlour

Christopher's First Poem

My name is Christopher and I go to preschool,

My best friend is Jack, who is really cool.

I watch Fireman Sam on TV,

Playing with my kitchen is lots of fun for me.

I just love tomato pasta to eat,

And sometimes chocolate yoghurts for a treat.

Red is a colour I like a lot,

My Marshall Zoomer is the best present I ever got.

My favourite person is Ciara, who is a gem,

So this, my first poem, is just for them!

Christopher Millsopp (3)

Knockando Playgroup, Aberlour

Harry's First Poem

My name is Harry and I go to preschool,
My best friend is Jack, who is really cool.
I watch Messy Goes to Okido on TV,
Playing with my tractor is lots of fun for me.
I just love noodles to eat,
And sometimes chocolate for a treat.
Red is a colour I like a lot,
My ukulele is the best present I ever got.
My favourite person is Archie, who is a gem,
So this, my first poem, is just for them!

Harry Meikle (4)
Knockando Playgroup, Aberlour

Thorsten's First Poem

My name is Thorsten and I go to preschool,

My best friend is Angus, who is really cool.

I watch Ice Age on TV,

Playing jigsaws is lots of fun for me.

I just love porridge to eat,

And sometimes chocolate for a treat.

Yellow is a colour I like a lot,

My tree cutter is the best present I ever got.

My favourite person is Aigen, my doggy, who is a gem,

So this, my first poem, is just for them!

Thorsten Baird (3)

Knockando Playgroup, Aberlour

Jack's First Poem

My name is Jack and I go to preschool,
My best friend is Jodie, who is really cool.
I watch Peter Rabbit on TV,
Playing with my tractors is lots of fun for me.
I just love raspberries to eat,
And sometimes chocolate for a treat.
Pink is a colour I like a lot,
My bike is the best present I ever got.
My favourite person is Mum, who is a gem,
So this, my first poem, is just for them!

Jack Flesh (4)

Knockando Playgroup, Aberlour

Sam's First Poem

My name is Sam and I go to preschool,

My best friend is Jack, who is really cool.

I watch PAW Patrol on TV,

Playing music is lots of fun for me.

I just love pasta to eat,

And sometimes ice cream for a treat.

Purple is a colour I like a lot,

My Marshall puppy is the best present I ever got.

My favourite person is Mummy, who is a gem,

So this, my first poem, is just for them!

Sam William Packham (3)

Knockando Playgroup, Aberlour

Finlay's First Poem

My name is **Finlay** and I go to preschool,
My best friend is **Nicola**, who is really cool.
I watch **PAW Patrol** on TV,
Playing **puzzles** is lots of fun for me.
I just love **pizza** to eat,
And sometimes **cake** for a treat.
Blue is a colour I like a lot,
My **accordion** is the best present I ever got.
My favourite person is **Dad**, who is a gem,
So this, my first poem, is just for them!

Finlay Meldrum (3)
Knockando Playgroup, Aberlour

Samuel's First Poem

My name is **Samuel** and I go to preschool,

My best friend is **Joseph**, who is really cool.

I watch **Thomas** on TV,

Playing **Thomas the Tank Engine** is lots of fun

for me.

I just love **apples** to eat,

And sometimes **chocolate stars** for a treat.

Red and blue are colours I like a lot,

My **Thomas with string with Annie and Clarabel** is the best present I ever got.

My favourite person is **Blake**, who is a gem,

So this, my first poem, is just for them!

Samuel Edwards (4)

Lossiemouth Childcare Centre, Lossiemouth

Henry's First Poem

My name is Henry and I go to preschool,

My best friend is Findlay, who is really cool.

I watch PAW Patrol on TV,

Playing with Transformers is lots of fun for me.

I just love macaroni to eat,

And sometimes chocolate for a treat.

Red is a colour I like a lot,

My PAW Patrol is the best present I ever got.

My favourite people are Mummy, Daddy and Edward, who are gems,

So this, my first poem, is just for them!

Henry Duncan Lambert (3)

Lossiemouth Childcare Centre, Lossiemouth

Angus' First Poem

My name is Angus and I go to preschool,

My best friend is Max, who is really cool.

I watch Power Rangers on TV,

Playing with my Power Rangers is lots of fun

for me.

I just love sandwiches to eat,

And sometimes jelly babies for a treat.

Pink is a colour I like a lot,

My cars and Transformer dinosaur are the best

presents I ever got.

My favourite person is Mummy, who is a gem,

So this, my first poem, is just for them!

Angus Michael Elliott (4)

Lossiemouth Childcare Centre, Lossiemouth

Finlay's First Poem

My name is Finlay and I go to preschool,

My best friend is Archie, who is really cool.

I watch PAW Patrol on TV,

Playing with my PAW Patrol is lots of fun for me.

I just love cookies to eat,

And sometimes chocolate for a treat.

Orange is a colour I like a lot,

My dragon dressing up is the best present I

ever got.

My favourite people are Mummy and Daddy, who

are gems,

So this, my first poem, is just for them!

Finlay Dodds (4)

Lossiemouth Childcare Centre, Lossiemouth

Maya's First Poem

My name is Maya and I go to preschool,
My best friend is Jack, who is really cool.
I watch Trolls on TV,
Playing Pig Goes Pop is lots of fun for me.
I just love chocolate sweet roll to eat,
And sometimes sweeties for a treat.
Pink is a colour I like a lot,
My Poppy is the best present I ever got.
My favourite people are Mummy, Daddy and my
baby brother, who are gems,
So this, my first poem, is just for them!

Maya Natasha Herrity (4)

Lossiemouth Childcare Centre, Lossiemouth

Harley's First Poem

My name is Harley and I go to preschool,

My best friends are Mummy and Cody, who are

really cool.

I watch dragons on TV,

Playing with dragons is lots of fun for me.

I just love sausage rolls to eat,

And sometimes cake and sweeties for a treat.

Green is a colour I like a lot,

My Polly Pockets are the best present I ever got.

My favourite person is Cody, who is a gem,

So this, my first poem, is just for them!

Harley James (3)
Lossiemouth Childcare Centre, Lossiemouth

Jack's First Poem

My name is Jack and I go to preschool,

My best friend is Archie, who is really cool.

I watch Spider-Man on TV,

Playing Transformers is lots of fun for me.

I just love sweetcorn and tuna sandwiches
to eat,

And sometimes a big lolly for a treat.

Orange is a colour I like a lot,

My dinosaurs are the best present I ever got.

My favourite person is Paige, who is a gem,

So this, my first poem, is just for them!

Jack Moore (4)

Lossiemouth Childcare Centre, Lossiemouth

Lucy's First Poem

My name is Lucy and I go to preschool,

My best friend is Nieve, who is really cool.

I watch Power Rangers on TV,

Playing with doggies is lots of fun for me.

I just love sandwiches and grapes to eat,

And sometimes KitKats for a treat.

Pink is a colour I like a lot,

My pirate ship is the best present I ever got.

My favourite people are Mummy and Daddy, who are gems,

So this, my first poem, is just for them!

Lucy Connie Jackson (3)
Lossiemouth Childcare Centre, Lossiemouth

Koa's First Poem

My name is Koa and I go to preschool,

My best friend is Logan, who is really cool.

I watch PAW Patrol on TV,

Playing with Lego blocks is lots of fun for me.

I just love yoghurts to eat,

And sometimes cake for a treat.

Red is a colour I like a lot,

My chocolate is the best present I ever got.

My favourite people are Mummy and Daddy, who

are gems,

So this, my first poem, is just for them!

Koa Fenwick (3)

Lossiemouth Childcare Centre, Lossiemouth

Harrison's First Poem

My name is **Harrison** and I go to preschool,
My best friend is **Joseph**, who is really cool.
I watch **Power Rangers** on TV,
Playing **with my new camera** is lots of fun for me.
I just love **cake** to eat,
And sometimes **chocolate** for a treat.
Blue is a colour I like a lot,
My **superhero toys** are the best present I ever got.
My favourite person is **Abigail**, who is a gem,
So this, my first poem, is just for them!

Harrison Jack May (4)

Lossiemouth Childcare Centre, Lossiemouth

Katie's First Poem

My name is **Katie** and I go to preschool,

My best friends are **Mummy and Alfie**, who are

really cool.

I watch **Frozen** on TV,

Playing **on the Xbox with my brother** is lots of

fun for me.

I just love **macaroni** to eat,

And sometimes **a lollipop** for a treat.

Pink is a colour I like a lot,

My **Poppy** is the best present I ever got.

My favourite person is **Mummy**, who is a gem,

So this, my first poem, is just for them!

Katie Louise Bell (4)

Lossiemouth Childcare Centre, Lossiemouth

Ellie's First Poem

My name is **Ellie** and I go to preschool,

My best friend is **Maya**, who is really cool.

I watch **Room on the Broom** on TV,

Playing **with my teddy, Pandy,** is lots of fun for me.

I just love **chicken nuggets** to eat,

And sometimes **sweeties** for a treat.

Red is a colour I like a lot,

My **Supergirl dress** is the best present I ever got.

My favourite person is **Maya**, who is a gem,

So this, my first poem, is just for them!

Ellie Iris Ralston (4)

Lossiemouth Childcare Centre, Lossiemouth

Freya's First Poem

My name is **Freya** and I go to preschool,

My best friend is **Ava**, who is really cool.

I watch **Marsha** on TV,

Playing **with my Polly Pockets** is lots of fun for me.

I just love **broccoli** to eat,

And sometimes **Smarties** for a treat.

Pink is a colour I like a lot,

My **unicorn** is the best present I ever got.

My favourite people are **Mummy and Daddy**, who are gems,

So this, my first poem, is just for them!

Freya Rose Gresswell Grant (4)

Lossiemouth Childcare Centre, Lossiemouth

Arran's First Poem

My name is **Arran** and I go to preschool,

My best friend is **Ryan**, who is really cool.

I watch **Pokémon** on TV,

Playing **Rescue PAW Patrol** is lots of fun for me.

I just love **chicken** to eat,

And sometimes **chocolate** for a treat.

Green is a colour I like a lot,

My **PAW Patrol** is the best present I ever got.

My favourite person is **Daddy**, who is a gem,

So this, my first poem, is just for them!

Arran Ritchie (3)
Lossiemouth Childcare Centre, Lossiemouth

Blake's First Poem

My name is **Blake** and I go to preschool,

My best friend is **Maya**, who is really cool.

I watch **Postman Pat** on TV,

Playing **with the trick box** is lots of fun for me.

I just love **chocolate sandwiches** to eat,

And sometimes **sweeties** for a treat.

Red is a colour I like a lot,

My **cars** are the best present I ever got.

My favourite person is **Samuel**, who is a gem,

So this, my first poem, is just for them!

Blake Philip (4)

Lossiemouth Childcare Centre, Lossiemouth

Joseph's First Poem

My name is Joseph and I go to preschool,

My best friend is Harrison, who is really cool.

I watch Spider-Man on TV,

Playing with Spider-Man toys is lots of fun for me.

I just love toast to eat,

And sometimes chocolate for a treat.

Pink is a colour I like a lot,

My Spider-Man is the best present I ever got.

My favourite person is Harrison, who is a gem,

So this, my first poem, is just for them!

Joseph McIntosh (4)

Lossiemouth Childcare Centre, Lossiemouth

Lily's First Poem

My name is Lily and I go to preschool,

My best friend is Isla, who is really cool.

I watch Alice in Wonderland on TV,

Playing with butterflies is lots of fun for me.

I just love chicken to eat,

And sometimes ice cream for a treat.

Purple is a colour I like a lot,

My toys are the best present I ever got.

My favourite person is Mummy, who is a gem,

So this, my first poem, is just for them!

Lily Robinson (3)

Lossiemouth Childcare Centre, Lossiemouth

Nieve's First Poem

My name is Nieve and I go to preschool,
My best friend is Jessica, who is really cool.
I watch My Little Pony on TV,
Playing with my ponies is lots of fun for me.
I just love chicken nuggets to eat,
And sometimes Smarties for a treat.
Purple is a colour I like a lot,
My doggy is the best present I ever got.
My favourite person is Daddy, who is a gem,
So this, my first poem, is just for them!

Nieve Elizabeth Smith (4)

Lossiemouth Childcare Centre, Lossiemouth

Harry's First Poem

My name is **Harry** and I go to preschool,

My best friend is **Archie**, who is really cool.

I watch **Thomas** on TV,

Playing **cars** is lots of fun for me.

I just love **cheese toasties** to eat,

And sometimes **ice cream** for a treat.

Orange is a colour I like a lot,

My **garage and cars** are the best presents I ever got.

My favourite person is **Gran**, who is a gem,

So this, my first poem, is just for them!

Harry Williams (4)

Lossiemouth Childcare Centre, Lossiemouth

Ava's First Poem

My name is Ava and I go to preschool,
My best friend is Maya, who is really cool.
I watch Trolls on TV,
Playing with my little horse is lots of fun for me.
I just love banana to eat,
And sometimes a Kinder egg for a treat.
Black is a colour I like a lot,
My Twilight Sparkle is the best present I ever got.
My favourite person is Mummy, who is a gem,
So this, my first poem, is just for them!

Ava Lynne Midgley (4)
Lossiemouth Childcare Centre, Lossiemouth

Isla's First Poem

My name is Isla and I go to preschool,

My best friend is Lily, who is really cool.

I watch My Little Pony on TV,

Playing Barbies is lots of fun for me.

I just love cheese to eat,

And sometimes sweeties for a treat.

Blue is a colour I like a lot,

My Rainbow Dash toothbrush is the best present

I ever got.

My favourite person is Mummy, who is a gem,

So this, my first poem, is just for them!

Isla Jayne Simpson (4)

Lossiemouth Childcare Centre, Lossiemouth

Jack's First Poem

My name is Jack and I go to preschool,
My best friend is Lily, who is really cool.
I watch Minions on TV,
Playing on my scooter is lots of fun for me.
I just love spaghetti Bolognese to eat,
And sometimes a lollipop for a treat.
Blue is a colour I like a lot,
My Iron Man is the best present I ever got.
My favourite person is Daddy, who is a gem,
So this, my first poem, is just for them!

Jack Dobson (3)
Lossiemouth Childcare Centre, Lossiemouth

Lilja's First Poem

My name is **Lilja** and I go to preschool,

My best friend is **Katie Bell**, who is really cool.

I watch **Dora the Explorer** on TV,

Playing **with Moosy** is lots of fun for me.

I just love **ham** to eat,

And sometimes **ice cream** for a treat.

Pink is a colour I like a lot,

My **Moosy** is the best present I ever got.

My favourite person is **Katie Bell**, who is a gem,

So this, my first poem, is just for them!

Lilja Gowanlock (4)

Lossiemouth Childcare Centre, Lossiemouth

Ellie's First Poem

My name is Ellie and I go to preschool,
My best friend is Lacey, who is really cool.
I watch Mickey Mouse on TV,
Playing puzzles is lots of fun for me.
I just love chicken nuggets to eat,
And sometimes yoghurt for a treat.
Purple is a colour I like a lot,
My Poppy dress is the best present I ever got.
My favourite person is Lacey, who is a gem,
So this, my first poem, is just for them!

Ellie Handford (4)

Lossiemouth Childcare Centre, Lossiemouth

Leo's First Poem

My name is Leo and I go to preschool,
My best friend is Koa, who is really cool.
I watch Topsy and Tim on TV,
Playing on my bike is lots of fun for me.
I just love macaroni cheese to eat,
And sometimes a trip to Pinz for a treat.
Blue is a colour I like a lot,
My toy car is the best present I ever got.
My favourite person is Mum, who is a gem,
So this, my first poem, is just for them!

Leo Morton (3)

Lossiemouth Childcare Centre, Lossiemouth

Isabella's First Poem

My name is **Isabella** and I go to preschool,
My best friend is **Ellie**, who is really cool.
I watch **PAW Patrol** on TV,
Playing **with trains** is lots of fun for me.
I just love **fish fingers** to eat,
And sometimes **ice cream** for a treat.
Orange is a colour I like a lot,
My **baby** is the best present I ever got.
My favourite person is **Ellie**, who is a gem,
So this, my first poem, is just for them!

Isabella Gandy (4)

Lossiemouth Childcare Centre, Lossiemouth

Jessica's First Poem

My name is Jessica and I go to preschool,

My best friend is Nieve, who is really cool.

I watch Trolls on TV,

Playing with my Barbie dog is lots of fun for me.

I just love apples to eat,

And sometimes Smarties for a treat.

Pink is a colour I like a lot,

My Shopkins are the best present I ever got.

My favourite person is Mummy, who is a gem,

So this, my first poem, is just for them!

Jessica Murray (3)

Lossiemouth Childcare Centre, Lossiemouth

Oscar's First Poem

My name is Oscar and I go to preschool,

My best friend is Evan, who is really cool.

I watch Blaze on TV,

Playing with bouncy balls is lots of fun for me.

I just love sausages to eat,

And sometimes marshmallows for a treat.

Green is a colour I like a lot,

My toy box is the best present I ever got.

My favourite person is Evan, who is a gem,

So this, my first poem, is just for them!

Oscar Renison (4)

Lossiemouth Childcare Centre, Lossiemouth

Max's First Poem

My name is **Max** and I go to preschool,

My best friend is **Aiden**, who is really cool.

I watch **Star Wars** on TV,

Playing **pirates** is lots of fun for me.

I just love **cheese pasta** to eat,

And sometimes **chocolate** for a treat.

Blue is a colour I like a lot,

My **Star Wars Lego** is the best present I ever got.

My favourite person is **Lily**, who is a gem,

So this, my first poem, is just for them!

Max Wainwright (3)

Lossiemouth Childcare Centre, Lossiemouth

Ryan's First Poem

My name is **Ryan** and I go to preschool,
My best friend is **Arran**, who is really cool.
I watch **Trolls** on TV,
Playing **Pokémon** is lots of fun for me.
I just love **fish finger** to eat,
And sometimes **sweeties** for a treat.
Yellow is a colour I like a lot,
My **Pikachu** is the best present I ever got.
My favourite person is **Dad**, who is a gem,
So this, my first poem, is just for them!

Ryan Denoon (3)
Lossiemouth Childcare Centre, Lossiemouth

Archie's First Poem

My name is **Archie** and I go to preschool,

My best friend is **Harris**, who is really cool.

I watch **Trolls** on TV,

Playing **making models** is lots of fun for me.

I just love **cheese** to eat,

And sometimes **sweeties** for a treat.

Blue is a colour I like a lot,

My **dragon** is the best present I ever got.

My favourite person is **Daddy**, who is a gem,

So this, my first poem, is just for them!

Archie Dempsey (3)
Lossiemouth Childcare Centre, Lossiemouth

Lacey's First Poem

My name is Lacey and I go to preschool,
My best friend is Joshua, who is really cool.
I watch Else and Anna on TV,
Playing puzzles is lots of fun for me.
I just love bananas to eat,
And sometimes yoghurt for a treat.
Blue is a colour I like a lot,
My Elsa is the best present I ever got.
My favourite person is Joshua, who is a gem,
So this, my first poem, is just for them!

Lacey Jane Goodwin (4)
Lossiemouth Childcare Centre, Lossiemouth

Logan's First Poem

My name is Logan and I go to preschool,
My best friend is Mummy, who is really cool.
I watch Justin on TV,
Playing with nee naws is lots of fun for me.
I just love popcorn to eat,
And sometimes sweeties for a treat.
Green is a colour I like a lot,
My toys are the best present I ever got.
My favourite person is Mummy, who is a gem,
So this, my first poem, is just for them!

Logan Cooper (3)
Lossiemouth Childcare Centre, Lossiemouth

Joshua's First Poem

My name is Joshua and I go to preschool,

My best friend is Sam, who is really cool.

I watch Fireman Sam on TV,

Playing Batman is lots of fun for me.

I just love apples to eat,

And sometimes sweets for a treat.

Blue is a colour I like a lot,

My PAW Patrol is the best present I ever got.

My favourite person is Mum, who is a gem,

So this, my first poem, is just for them!

Joshua Joyce (3)

Lossiemouth Childcare Centre, Lossiemouth

Archie's First Poem

My name is Archie and I go to preschool,
My best friend is Joshua, who is really cool.
I watch PAW Patrol on TV,
Playing jigsaws is lots of fun for me.
I just love sausages to eat,
And sometimes cake for a treat.
Green is a colour I like a lot,
My Lego is the best present I ever got.
My favourite person is Evan, who is a gem,
So this, my first poem, is just for them!

Archie Griffiths (4)
Lossiemouth Childcare Centre, Lossiemouth

Aiden's First Poem

My name is Aiden and I go to preschool,

My best friend is Max, who is really cool.

I watch bears on TV,

Playing Avengers is lots of fun for me.

I just love pizza to eat,

And sometimes chocolate for a treat.

Red is a colour I like a lot,

My big robot is the best present I ever got.

My favourite person is Max, who is a gem,

So this, my first poem, is just for them!

Aiden Johnstone (4)

Lossiemouth Childcare Centre, Lossiemouth

Amber's First Poem

My name is **Amber** and I go to preschool,
My best friend is **Aoife**, who is really cool.
I watch **PAW Patrol** on TV,
Playing **with Sleepy Bear** is lots of fun for me.
I just love **all coloured peppers** to eat,
And sometimes **lollipop** for a treat.
Pink and purple are colours I like a lot,
My **pink penguin, Waddly** is the best present I
ever got.
My favourite person is **Dylan, my big brother**, who
is a gem,
So this, my first poem, is just for them!

Amber Swanson (3)

Pitreavie Playgroup, Dunfermline

Matthew's First Poem

My name is **Matthew** and I go to preschool,

My best friends are **Chloe and Charlotte**, who are really cool.

I watch **PAW Patrol** on TV,

Playing **with my air rider** is lots of fun for me.

I just love **cheese sandwich** to eat,

And sometimes **pasta** for a treat.

Orange is a colour I like a lot,

The present Emmi got me is the best present I ever got.

My favourite person is **Cayla**, who is a gem,

So this, my first poem, is just for them!

Matthew Douglas Codona (4)
Pitreavie Playgroup, Dunfermline

Charlotte's First Poem

My name is Charlotte and I go to preschool,
My best friend is Amy, who is really cool.
I watch Peppa Pig on TV,
Playing with the doll is lots of fun for me.
I just love fish to eat,
And sometimes sweeties for a treat.
Yellow is a colour I like a lot,
My Peppa Pig toy is the best present I ever got.
My favourite people are Mum, Dad and Maia, who
are gems,
So this, my first poem, is just for them!

Charlotte Harker (2)
Pitreavie Playgroup, Dunfermline

Amelia's First Poem

My name is Amelia and I go to preschool,
My best friend is Zoe, who is really cool.
I watch The Lion Guard on TV,
Playing with stones is lots of fun for me.
I just love banana to eat,
And sometimes candyfloss for a treat.
Pink is a colour I like a lot,
My sticker book is the best present I ever got.
My favourite person is Aoife, who is a gem,
So this, my first poem, is just for them!

Amelia Sallnow (3)
Pitreavie Playgroup, Dunfermline

Euan's First Poem

My name is **Euan** and I go to preschool,
My best friend is **Kristie**, who is really cool.
I watch **PAW Patrol** on TV,
Playing **in my room** is lots of fun for me.
I just love **my mum's soup** to eat,
And sometimes **apples** for a treat.
Red is a colour I like a lot,
My **dinosaur** is the best present I ever got.
My favourite person is **Mummy**, who is a gem,
So this, my first poem, is just for them!

Euan Love (3)

Pitreavie Playgroup, Dunfermline

Arran's First Poem

My name is Arran and I go to preschool,

My best friend is Brodie, who is really cool.

I watch Blaze and the Monster Machines on TV,

Playing monster trucks and trains with my big brother Lachlan is lots of fun for me.

I just love corn on the cob and fish fingers and chips to eat,

And sometimes ice cream cone and sweeties for a treat.

Yellow is a colour I like a lot,

My football is the best present I ever got.

My favourite person is my big brother Lachlan, who is a gem,

So this, my first poem, is just for them!

Arran Stewart McGeachie (2)

Torphins Playgroup, Banchory

Brodie's First Poem

My name is Brodie and I go to preschool,

My best friend is my sister Ella, who is really cool.

I watch Tractor Tom, Tractor Ted and Peppa Pig on TV,

Playing with my tractors, especially my John Deere one, is lots of fun for me.

I just love mince, tatties and peas to eat,

And sometimes chocolate buttons for a treat.

Green is a colour I like a lot,

My John Deere tractor is the best present I ever got.

My favourite person is Granda Glassel, who is a gem,

So this, my first poem, is just for them!

Brodie Davidson (2)

Torphins Playgroup, Banchory

Charlotte's First Poem

My name is Charlotte and I go to playschool,
Zara's my best friend, and she's really cool.
I like watching Peppa on TV,
Playing Gonna Get You is lots of fun for me.
I just love pasta and meatballs to eat,
And sometimes chocolate froggies for a treat.
Green is a colour I like a lot,
My spinning top is the best present I ever got.
My favourite person is Mumma, who is a gem,
So this, my first poem, is just for them!

Charlotte Lockwood (3)

Torphins Playgroup, Banchory

Findlay's First Poem

My name is Findlay and I go to preschool,
My best friend is Phoebe, who is really cool.
I watch Thomas the Tank Engine on TV,
Playing with my train set is lots of fun for me.
I just love spaghetti Bolognese to eat,
And sometimes fish and chips for a treat.
Pink is a colour I like a lot,
My balance bike is the best present I ever got.
My favourite person is Auntie Sue, who is a gem,
So this, my first poem, is just for them!

Findlay Boyd (2)
Torphins Playgroup, Banchory

Imogen's First Poem

My name is Imogen and I go to preschool,
My best friend is Eloise, who is really cool.
I watch Bing and Twirlywoos on TV,
Playing with my doll Harry is lots of fun for me.
I just love bagels and crackers to eat,
And sometimes chocolate for a treat.
Blue is a colour I like a lot,
My Makka Pakka is the best present I ever got.
My favourite person is Marissa, who is a gem,
So this, my first poem, is just for them!

Imogen Robertson (2)

Torphins Playgroup, Banchory

Zara's First Poem

My name is **Zara** and I go to preschool,

My best friends are **Charlotte and Daisy**, who are really cool.

I watch **My Little Pony** on TV,

Playing **dressing up** is lots of fun for me.

I just love **macaroni** to eat,

And sometimes **ice lollies** for a treat.

Pink is a colour I like a lot,

My **dolly** is the best present I ever got.

My favourite person is **Daddy**, who is a gem,

So this, my first poem, is just for them!

Zara Shepherd (3)

Torphins Playgroup, Banchory

Daisy's First Poem

My name is Daisy and I go to preschool,

My best friend is Zara, who is really cool.

I watch Peppa Pig on TV,

Playing Barbies is lots of fun for me.

I just love carrots, sausages and pepperoni pizza to eat,

And sometimes sweeties for a treat.

Pink is a colour I like a lot,

My toy kitchen is the best present I ever got.

My favourite person is Olly, who is a gem,

So this, my first poem, is just for them!

Daisy Eleanor Newman (3)

Torphins Playgroup, Banchory

Kian's First Poem

My name is **Kian** and I go to preschool,

My best friends are **Mummy and Daddy**, who are

really cool.

I watch **PAW Patrol** on TV,

Playing **football** is lots of fun for me.

I just love **strawberries** to eat,

And sometimes **ice cream** for a treat.

Red is a colour I like a lot,

My **scooter** is the best present I ever got.

My favourite person is **Granny B**, who is a gem,

So this, my first poem, is just for them!

Kian Allan (3)

Torphins Playgroup, Banchory

Fergus' First Poem

My name is Fergus and I go to preschool,

My best friend is Calum, who is really cool.

I watch dinosaurs on TV,

Playing diggers is lots of fun for me.

I just love cheese to eat,

And sometimes chocolate for a treat.

Blue is a colour I like a lot,

My stomping T-rex is the best present I ever got.

My favourite person is Mummy, who is a gem,

So this, my first poem, is just for them!

Fergus McCallum (2)

Torphins Playgroup, Banchory

Eloise's First Poem

My name is Eloise and I go to preschool,

My best friend is Katie, who is really cool.

I watch Cinderella on TV,

Playing on my bike is lots of fun for me.

I just love toast to eat,

And sometimes a sweetie for a treat.

Blue is a colour I like a lot,

My Elsa dress is the best present I ever got.

My favourite person is Mummy, who is a gem,

So this, my first poem, is just for them!

Eloise Fulton (2)

Torphins Playgroup, Banchory

Jessica's First Poem

My name is Jessica and I go to preschool,
My best friend is Rosie, who is really cool.
I watch Peppa Pig on TV,
Playing with my buggy is lots of fun for me.
I just love pasta to eat,
And sometimes apples for a treat.
Pink is a colour I like a lot,
My baby is the best present I ever got.
My favourite person is Freya, who is a gem,
So this, my first poem, is just for them!

Jessica Gray (2)

Torphins Playgroup, Banchory

Callum's First Poem

My name is Callum and I go to preschool,
My best friend is Daisy, who is really cool.
I watch PAW Patrol on TV,
Playing diggers is lots of fun for me.
I just love tuna to eat,
And sometimes croissants for a treat.
Orange is a colour I like a lot,
My Zoomer is the best present I ever got.
My favourite person is Mum, who is a gem,
So this, my first poem, is just for them!

Callum Jamie Yule (3)
Torphins Playgroup, Banchory

My First Poem

We hope you have enjoyed reading this book – and that you will continue to enjoy it in the coming years.

If you're a young writer who enjoys reading and creative writing, or the parent of an enthusiastic poet or story writer, do visit our websites, www.myfirstpoem.com and www.youngwriters.co.uk. Here you will find free competitions, workshops and games, as well as recommended reads, a poetry glossary and our blog.

If you would like to order further copies of this book, or any of our other titles, then please give us a call or visit www.myfirstpoem.com.

My First Poem
Remus House
Coltsfoot Drive
Peterborough
PE2 9BF

Tel: 01733 898110
info@myfirstpoem.com